AF407435

TRUMPED

Published 2024
Classic Books

Trumped

The Wit and Wisdom of Donald J. Trump

INTRODUCTION

In the tumultuous landscape of modern American politics, few figures have ignited as much fervor, controversy, and curiosity as Donald J. Trump, the 45th President of the United States. From his iconic catchphrases to his unfiltered Twitter pronouncements, Trump has left an indelible mark on the public consciousness, captivating audiences with his unique brand of rhetoric and unapologetic demeanor.

In this collection, we embark on a journey through the vivid tapestry of Trumpian language—a tapestry woven with bold proclamations, blistering criticisms, and unabashed self-promotion. Here, within these pages, lie the words that have defined an era, offering insight into the mind of a man who reshaped the political landscape and challenged conventions at every turn.

Spanning his decades-long career as a real estate mogul, television personality, and ultimately, Commander-in-Chief, these quotes encapsulate the essence of Trump— the businessman, the entertainer, and the statesman. Whether delivered from the podium of a political rally, the boardroom of Trump Tower, or the Oval Office itself, each utterance bears the unmistakable stamp of his persona: bold, brash, and unapologetically Trump.

But this collection is more than a mere anthology of soundbites. It is a testament to the power of language to shape perceptions, galvanize movements, and stir passions. Love him or loathe him, Trump's words have resonated with millions, sparking debates, fueling controversies, and leaving an indelible imprint on the fabric of American discourse.

As we delve into these quotes, let us not only marvel at their audacity and candor but also reflect on their implications for our society, our politics, and our collective future. For within these words lie not only the reflections of a single man, but also the reflections of a nation grappling with change, division, and the relentless march of history.

So join us as we unravel the Trump tapestry, exploring the highs and lows, the triumphs and tribulations, and the unforgettable moments that have defined the era of Trump. Whether you're a fervent supporter, a staunch critic, or simply an observer of history in the making, there's no denying the enduring impact of the words of Donald J. Trump.

Welcome to the world of Trump quotes—where controversy meets charisma, where politics meets entertainment, and where every utterance is a headline waiting to happen.

Enjoy the journey.

Everything in life is luck.

Donald Trump

The first thing the secretary types is the boss.

Donald Trump

As long as you're going to be thinking anyway,
think big.

Donald Trump

What separates the winners from the losers is how a person reacts to each new twist of fate.

Donald Trump

A little more moderation would be good. Of course, my life hasn't exactly been one of moderation.

Donald Trump

Do you mind if I sit back a little? Because your breath is very bad.

Donald Trump

The 1990's sure aren't like the 1980's.

Donald Trump

I like thinking big. If you're going to be thinking anything, you might as well think big.

Donald Trump

I don't make deals for the money. I've got enough, much more than I'll ever need. I do it to do it.

Donald Trump

Sometimes your best investments are the ones
you don't make.

Donald Trump

If you're going to be thinking, you may as well think big.

Donald Trump

You have to think anyway, so why not
think big?

Donald Trump

Experience taught me a few things. One is to listen to your gut, no matter how good something sounds on paper. The second is that you're generally better off sticking with what you know. And the third is that sometimes your best investments are the ones you don't make.

Donald Trump

The point is that you can't be too greedy.

Donald Trump

I'm a bit of a P. T. Barnum. I make stars out of everyone.

Donald Trump

Money was never a big motivation for me, except as a way to keep score. The real excitement is playing the game.

Donald Trump

I try to learn from the past, but I plan for the future by focusing exclusively on the present. That's where the fun is.

Donald Trump

Part of being a winner is knowing when enough is enough. Sometimes you have to give up the fight and walk away, and move on to something that's more productive.

Donald Trump

Every time you walk down the street people
are screaming, 'You're fired!'

Donald Trump

I wasn't satisfied just to earn a good living. I was looking to make a statement.

Donald Trump

Anyone who thinks my story is anywhere near over is sadly mistaken.

Donald Trump

I have made the tough decisions, always with an eye toward the bottom line. Perhaps it's time America was run like a business.

Donald Trump

I mean, there's no arguing. There is no anything. There is no beating around the bush. 'You're fired' is a very strong term.

Donald Trump

It's tangible, it's solid, it's beautiful. It's artistic, from my standpoint, and I just love real estate.

Donald Trump

One of the key problems today is that politics is such a disgrace, good people don't go into government.

Donald Trump

Well, real estate is always good, as far as I'm concerned.

Donald Trump

Well, yes, I've fired a lot of people. Generally I like other people to fire, because it's always a lousy task. But I have fired many people.

Donald Trump

Sometimes by losing a battle you find a new
way to win the war.

Donald Trump

Without passion you don't have energy, with out energy you have nothing.

Donald Trump

When somebody challenges you, fight back. Be brutal, be tough.

Donald Trump

I'm the No. 1 developer in New York, I'm the biggest in Atlantic City, and maybe we'll keep it that way.

Donald Trump

If you're interested in 'balancing' work and pleasure, stop trying to balance them. Instead make your work more pleasurable.

Donald Trump

I could never have imagined that firing 67 people on national television would actually make me more popular, especially with the younger generation.

Donald Trump

In the end, you're measured not by how much you undertake but by what you finally accomplish.

Donald Trump

That's one of the nice things. I mean, part of the beauty of me is that I'm very rich. So if I need $600 million, I can put $600 million myself. That's a huge advantage. I must tell you, that's a huge advantage over the other candidates.

Donald Trump

You know the funny thing, I don't get along with rich people. I get along with the middle class and the poor people better than I get along with the rich people.

Donald Trump

Well, I am a Republican, and I would run as a Republican. And I have a lot of confidence in the Republican Party. I don't have a lot of confidence in the president. I think what's happening to this country is unbelievably bad. We're no longer a respected country.

Donald Trump

If you look - look at - I mean, look at what's going on with your gasoline prices. They're going to go to $5, $6, $7 and we don't have anybody in Washington that calls OPEC and says, 'Fellas, it's time. It's over. You're not going to do it anymore.'

Donald Trump

The Arab League tells us to go in and take out Qaddafi. We've spent billions of dollars already with respect to the Arab League. Billions of dollars, because they told us to do it. Why aren't they paying for it? They don't like Qaddafi, Qaddafi's been a terrible thorn in their side.

Donald Trump

China gets their oil from Libya. Why isn't China involved? They're going out spending billions of dollars a day on trying to take over the world economically. And we're spending billions and billions and billions of dollars on policing the world. Why isn't China involved with Libya? That - we don't get oil from Libya, China does.

Donald Trump

I saw a report yesterday. There's so much oil, all over the world, they don't know where to dump it. And Saudi Arabia says, 'Oh, there's too much oil.' They - they came back yesterday. Did you see the report? They want to reduce oil production. Do you think they're our friends? They're not our friends.

Donald Trump

A certificate of live birth is not the same thing by any stretch of the imagination as a birth certificate.

Donald Trump

My big focus is China and OPEC and all of these countries that are just absolutely destroying the United States.

Donald Trump

Today, and I'm very strongly against tax increases.

Donald Trump

I support health care for people. I want people well taken care of. But I also want health care that we can afford as a country. I have people and friends closing down their businesses because of Obamacare.

Donald Trump

It's always good to be underestimated.

Donald Trump

I think Ronald Reagan was one of the great presidents, period, not just recently. I thought he had the demeanor. I thought he had the bearing. I thought he had the thought process.

Donald Trump

It's not like I'm anti-China. I just think it's ridiculous that we allow them to do what they're doing to this country, with the manipulation of the currency, that you write about and understand, and all of the other things that they do.

Donald Trump

But I believe in fair trade, and I will tell you, I have many, many friends heading up corporations, and people that do just business in China, they say it's virtually impossible. It's very, very hard to come into China. And yet, we welcome them with open arms.

Donald Trump

Getting things done in this country, if you want to build something, if you want to start a company, it's getting to be virtually impossible with all of the bureaucracy and all of the approvals.

Donald Trump

People might not think that, but the Republicans have all of the cards. And this is the time to get rid of Obamacare. This is the time to make the great deal.

Donald Trump

The debt limits have to come down. The whole world of debt has to be changed as far as this country is concerned. We have to create jobs and we have to create them rapidly because if we don't things are just going to head in a direction that's going to be almost impossible to recover from.

Donald Trump

So we really need jobs now. We have to take jobs away from other countries because other countries are taking our jobs. There is practically not a country that does business with the United States that isn't making - let's call it a very big profit. I mean China is going to make $300 billion on us at least this year.

Donald Trump

So Bush certainly wasn't the greatest, and Obama has not done the job. And he's created a lot of disincentive. He's created a lot of great dissatisfaction. Regulations and regulatory is going through the roof. It's almost impossible to get anything done in the country.

Donald Trump

I do have my ducks in line if I want to do it, but I'd love to see the Republicans pick somebody that was going to win and take over this country and frankly, to use the expression, 'Make America great again.'

Donald Trump

I think George Will is somebody that said recently that the Republicans will not lose, as a Republican, that the Republicans will not win the election. I think it was a terrible statement.

Donald Trump

A lot of people feel very good about Mitt Romney and I think he's going to do a great job.

Donald Trump

Mitt - what I speak to Mitt Romney about is jobs. What I speak to Mitt Romney about is China, because he's got a great view on China and how they're trying to destroy our country by taking our jobs and making our product and manipulating their currency, so that it makes it almost impossible for our companies to compete.

Donald Trump

Obama does not like the issue of where
he was born.

Donald Trump

It's a great thing when you can show that you've been successful and that you've made a lot of money and that you've employed a lot of people.

Donald Trump

I feel a lot of people listen to what I
have to say.

Donald Trump

We need a great president.

Donald Trump

I was a great student at a great school,
Wharton School of Finance.

Donald Trump

The Obama representatives like Robert Gibbs attack people viciously, but people like me will not be silent and will answer them back.

Donald Trump

Obama and his attack dogs have nothing but hate and anger in their hearts and spew it whenever possible.

Donald Trump

Obama has no solutions. Obama has failed the country and its great citizens, and they don't like it when somebody such as myself speaks the truth about this - it hurts too much.

Donald Trump

I think the big problem this country has is being politically correct. I've been challenged by so many people, and I don't frankly have time for total political correctness. And to be honest with you, this country doesn't have time either.

Donald Trump

We - we need strength, we need energy, we need quickness and we need brain in this country to turn it around.

Donald Trump

Our politicians are stupid. And the Mexican government is much smarter, much sharper, much more cunning. And they send the bad ones over because they don't want to pay for them. They don't want to take care of them. Why should they when the stupid leaders of the United States will do it for them?

Donald Trump

In July of 2004, I came out strongly against
the war with Iraq because it was going to
destabilize the Middle East.

Donald Trump

As far as single payer, it works in Canada. It works incredibly well in Scotland.

Donald Trump

I give to everybody. When they call, I give.
And do you know what? When I need
something from them two years later, three
years later, I call them, they are there for me.

Donald Trump

I have used the laws of this country just like the greatest people that you read about every day in business have used the laws of this country, the chapter laws, to do a great job for my company, for myself, for my employees, for my family, et cetera.

Donald Trump

Our military has to be strengthened. Our vets have to be taken care of. We have to end Obamacare, and we have to make our country great again, and I will do that.

Donald Trump

I have a great, great company. I employ thousands of people. And I'm very proud of the job I did.

Donald Trump

I am very, very proud to say that I am pro-life.

Donald Trump

I have a great relationship with the
Mexican people.

Donald Trump

Hillary Clinton is not going to be able to create jobs, I will tell you right now.

Donald Trump

Mexico's making a fortune off the
United States.

Donald Trump

I have an attention span that's as long as it has to be.

Donald Trump

Hillary Clinton was the worst Secretary
of State in the history of the country.
The world came apart under her reign as
Secretary of State.

Donald Trump

Politicians can't manage. All they can
do is talk.

Donald Trump

Saudi Arabia makes a billion dollars a day, okay? They make a billion dollars a day.

Donald Trump

If I were a liberal Democrat, people would say I'm the super genius of all time. The super genius of all time. If you're a conservative Republican, you've got to fight for your life. It's really an amazing thing.

Donald Trump

People love me. And you know what, I have been very successful. Everybody loves me.

Donald Trump

If I don't get along with Democrats, I'm sort of, like, out of business.

Donald Trump

I was a Democrat for a period of time early on. And then I was also an independent. And then I became a Republican.

Donald Trump

Somebody said I am the most popular person in Arizona because I am speaking the truth.

Donald Trump

You know that ISIS wants to go in and take over the Vatican? You have heard that. You know, that's a dream of theirs, to go into Italy.

Donald Trump

The Pope, I hope, can only be scared by God.

Donald Trump

I have great respect for the Pope. I like the
Pope. I actually like him.

Donald Trump

People are so shocked when they find... out I am Protestant. I am Presbyterian. And I go to church, and I love God, and I love my church.

Donald Trump

I played golf with my friends, and then I started to play with the hustlers. And I learned a lot. I learned about golf; I learned about gambling. I learned about everything.

Donald Trump

I own buildings. I'm a builder; I know how to build. Nobody can build like I can build. Nobody. And the builders in New York will tell you that. I build the best product. And my name helps a lot.

Donald Trump

Somebody made the statement that

Donald Trump

has built or owns the greatest collection of golf courses, ever, in the history of golf. And I believe that is 100 percent true.

Donald Trump

I've got the hottest brand in the world.

Donald Trump

I built a great company, one of the - some of the most iconic assets in the world, $10 billion of net worth, more than $10 billion of net worth, and frankly, I had a great time doing it.

Donald Trump

Private jets cost a lot of money.

Donald Trump

Iran is not getting rid of any of its nuclear plants. They're not getting rid of anything.

Donald Trump

Years ago, I predicted that Iran would take over Iraq. Iran and Iraq used to fight back and forth.

Donald Trump

The Iranians and Persians are excellent at the
art of negotiation.

Donald Trump

Many agree that the worst thing that could
ever happen is if Russia and China get closer.

Donald Trump

I don't like losers.

Donald Trump

The Veterans Administration is a scandal. It's corrupt, and what's going on is a disgrace. And, believe me, if I win, if I become president, that will end. The veterans will be treated properly.

Donald Trump

I deal with foreign countries. I made a lot of money dealing against China. I've made a lot of money dealing against many other countries.

Donald Trump

I have respect for Senator McCain. I used to like him a lot. I supported him. I raised a lot of money for his campaign against President Obama.

Donald Trump

I love Wisconsin. It's a great place.

Donald Trump

I have had lobbyists, and I have had some very good ones. They could do anything.

Donald Trump

I'm worth far too much money. I don't need anybody's money.

Donald Trump

I have very good executives and great children.
They're very good.

Donald Trump

So many people are on television that don't know me, and they're like experts on me.

Donald Trump

Obamacare is, number one and maybe least importantly, it's costing the country a fortune.

Donald Trump

If people can just pour into the country illegally, you don't have a country.

Donald Trump

Ronald Reagan became, you know, not only a Republican but a pretty conservative Republican - not the most. But a pretty conservative Republican. And he's somebody that I actually knew and liked. And he liked me. And I worked with him and helped him.

Donald Trump

I think that when you get right down to it, people do evolve on different issues. And, you know, I'm pro-life. And I was begrudgingly the other way.

Donald Trump

We've had soldiers that were so badly hurt and killed. I want their families to get something.

I went to the Wharton School of Finance, the toughest place to get into. I was a great student.

Donald Trump

I apologize when I'm wrong.

Donald Trump

We have to straighten out our country; we
have to make our country great again, and we
need energy and enthusiasm.

Donald Trump

I have women working in high positions. I was one of the first people to put women in charge of big construction jobs. And, you know, I've had a great relationship with women.

Donald Trump